Throughout the Forest

Written and Illustrated by
Joni Prew

Joni Prew
Circle Time Productions

Joni Prew
Circle Time Productions

All rights reserved.
No parts of this book may be reproduced, stored in a retrieval system, or transmitted in any form, by any means, including mechanical, electronic, photocopying, recording or otherwise without the prior consent of the author or publisher.

Published by Circle Time Productions
printed by KDP/Amazon
Words © 2024
Illustrations © 2024
ISBN: 979-8-9859710-5-7
BISAC: JNF003230/JNF003100

The forest is a large area filled with trees. Forests grow In many parts of the world.

Dedicated to animal lovers.

Throughout the forest
hiding among the tall grass
I spy a deer
that freezes as I pass

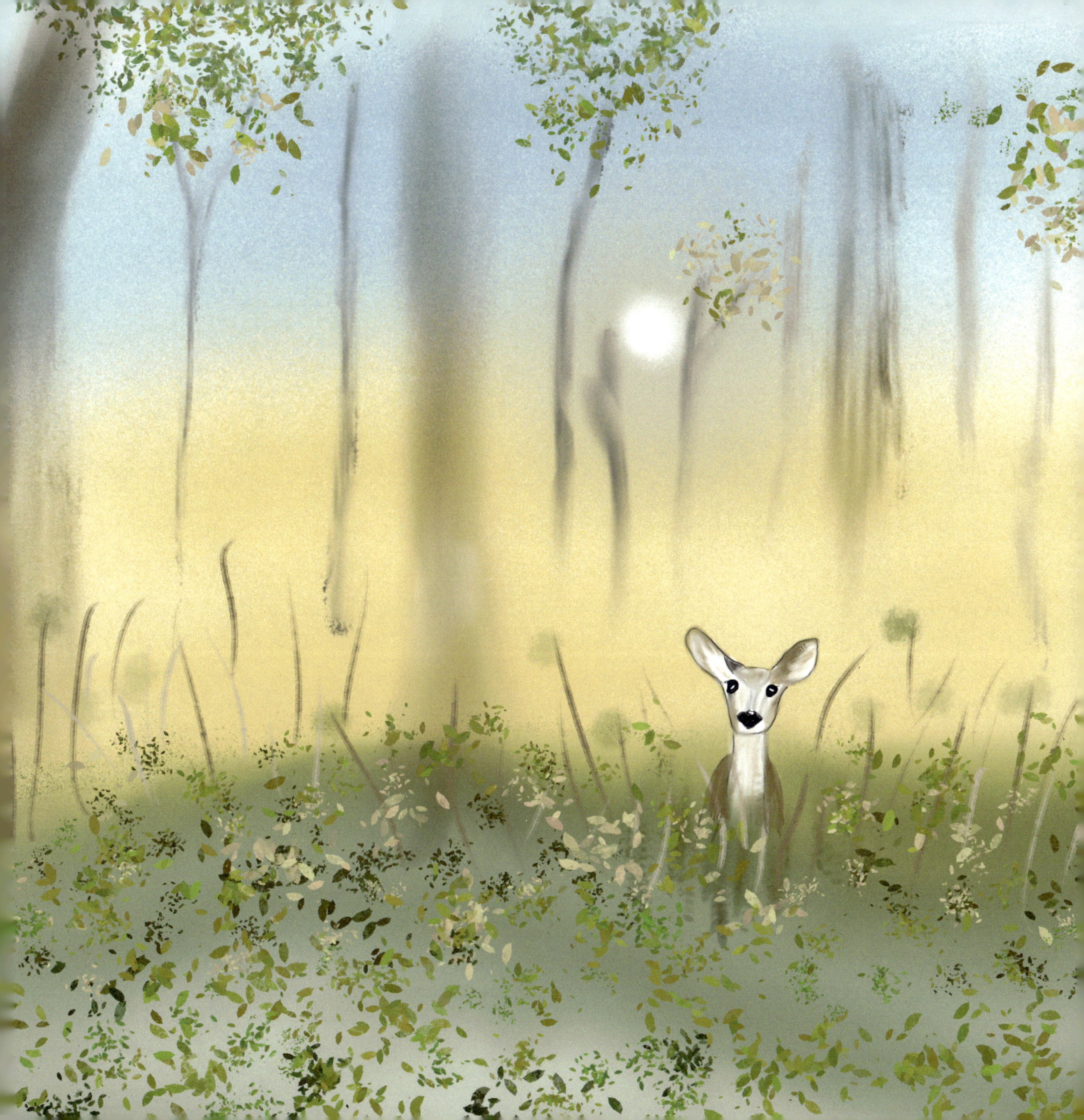

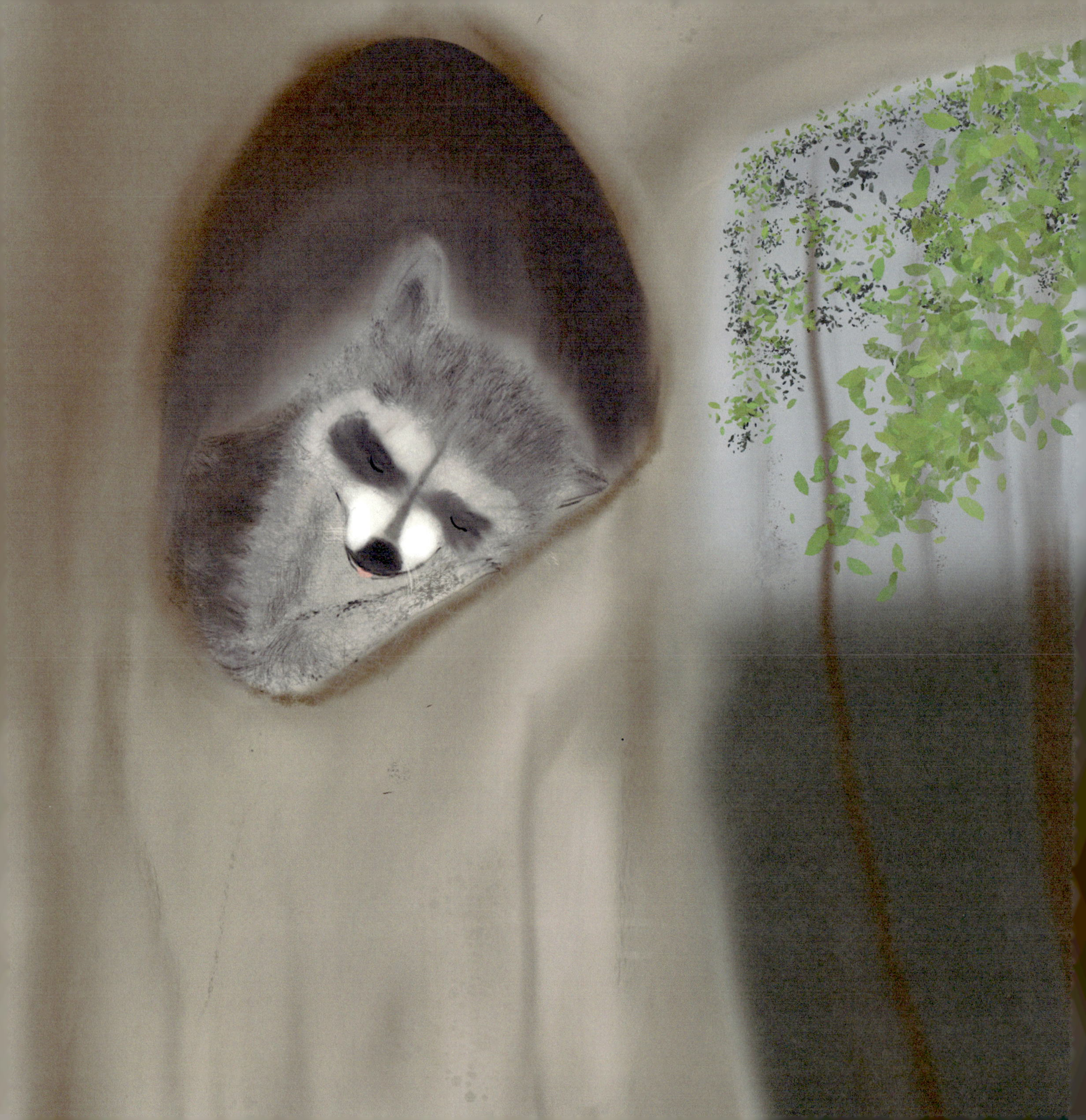

Throughout the forest sleeping

inside a tree

I spy a raccoon

she's a quiet as can be

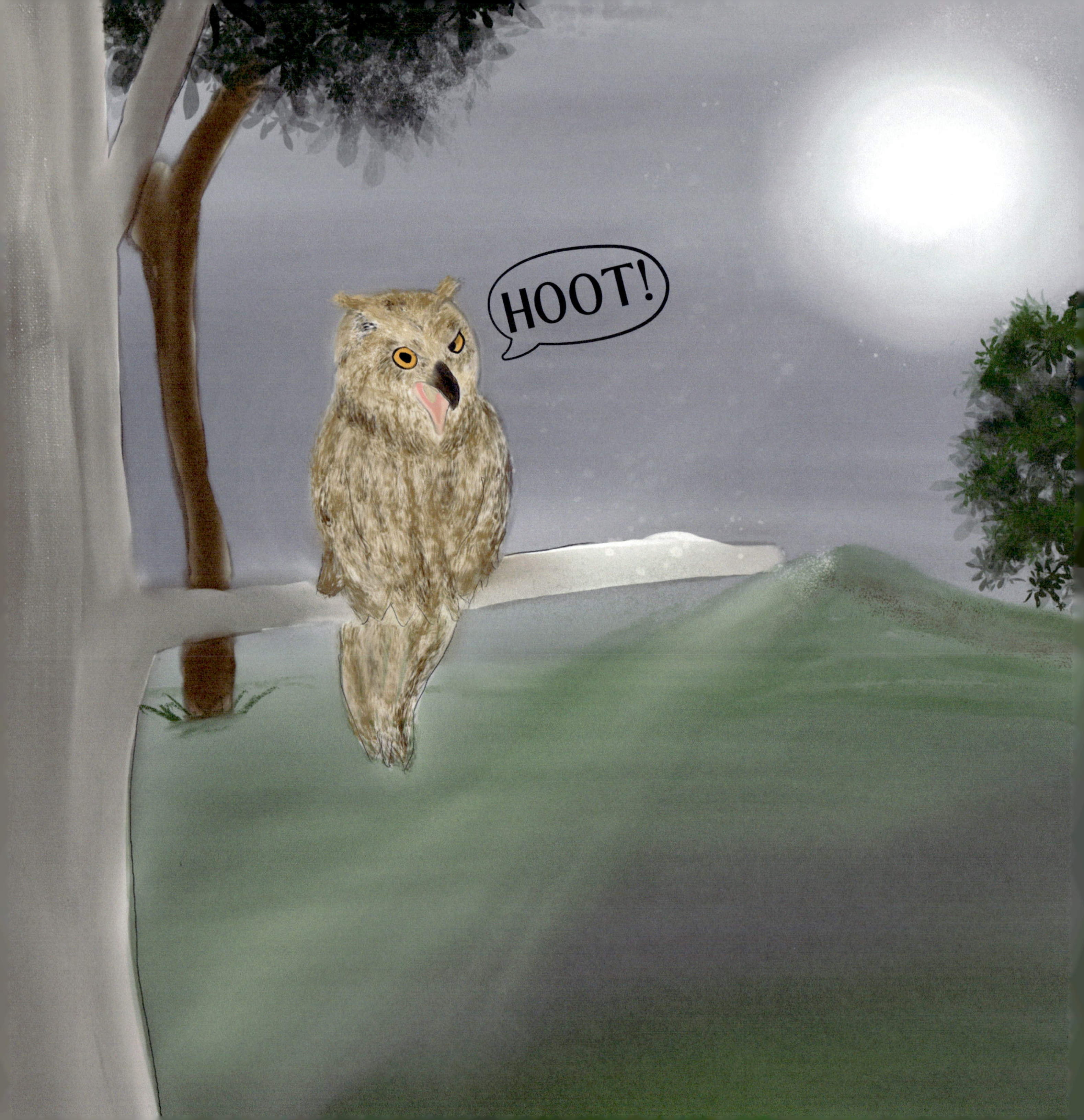
HOOT!

Throughout the forest
singing *by* the light of the moon
I spy an owl
hooting a happy tune

Throughout the forest rustling down in the leaves
I spy an opossum playing dead; such a tease

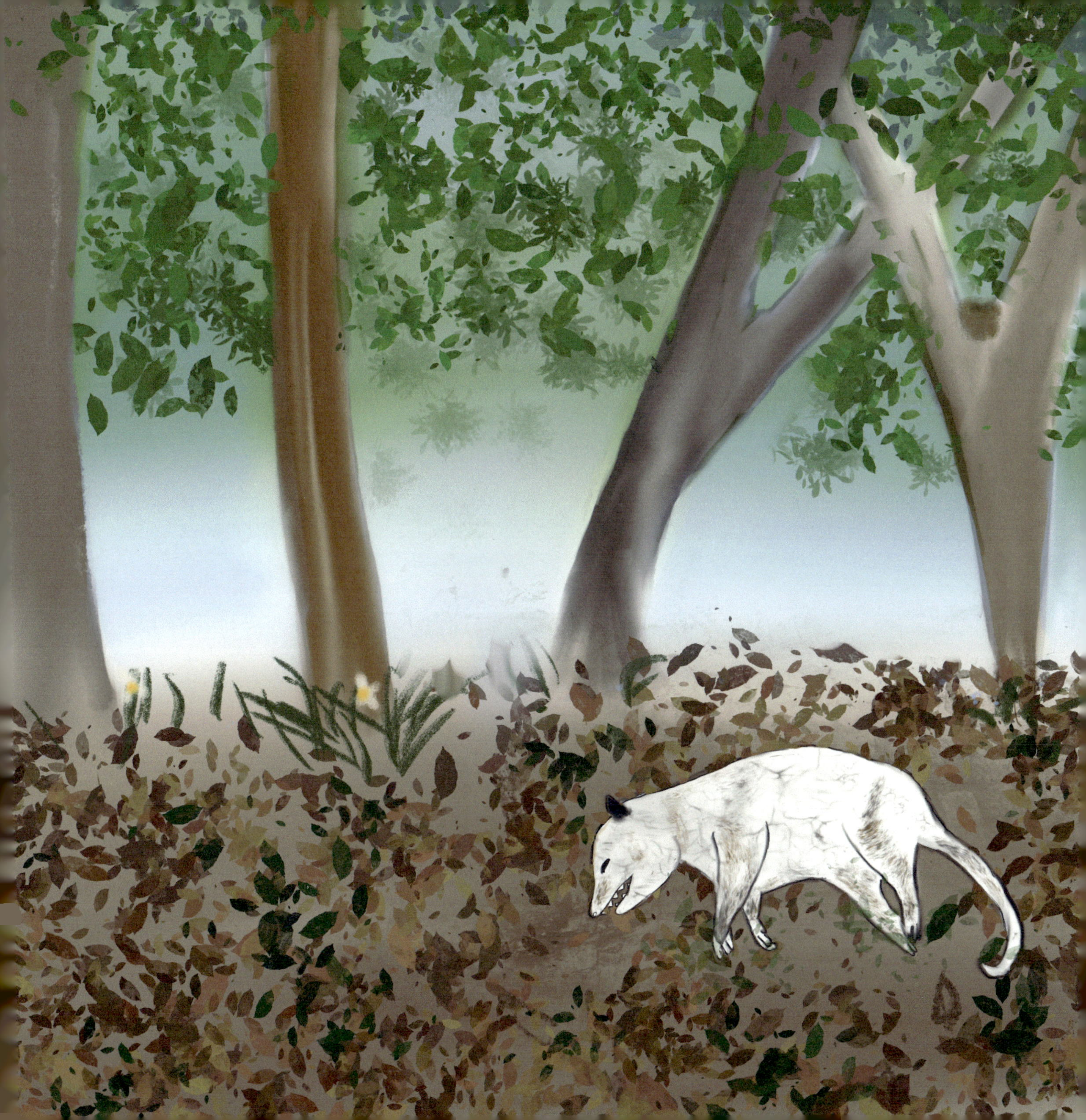

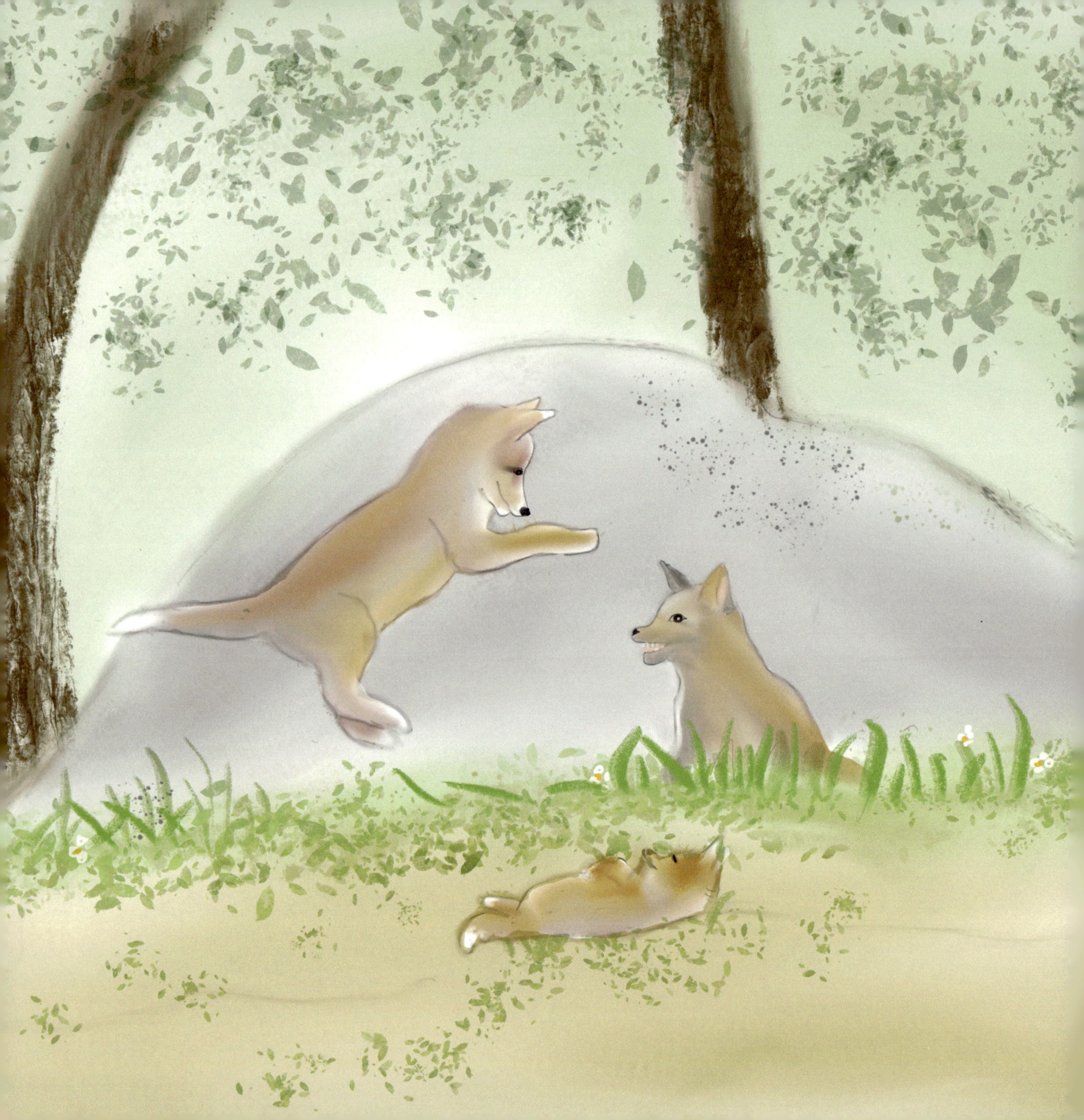

Throughout the forest running far away
I spy some fox
Who just want to play

Throughout the forest
lumbering up ahead
I spy a bear
heading off to bed

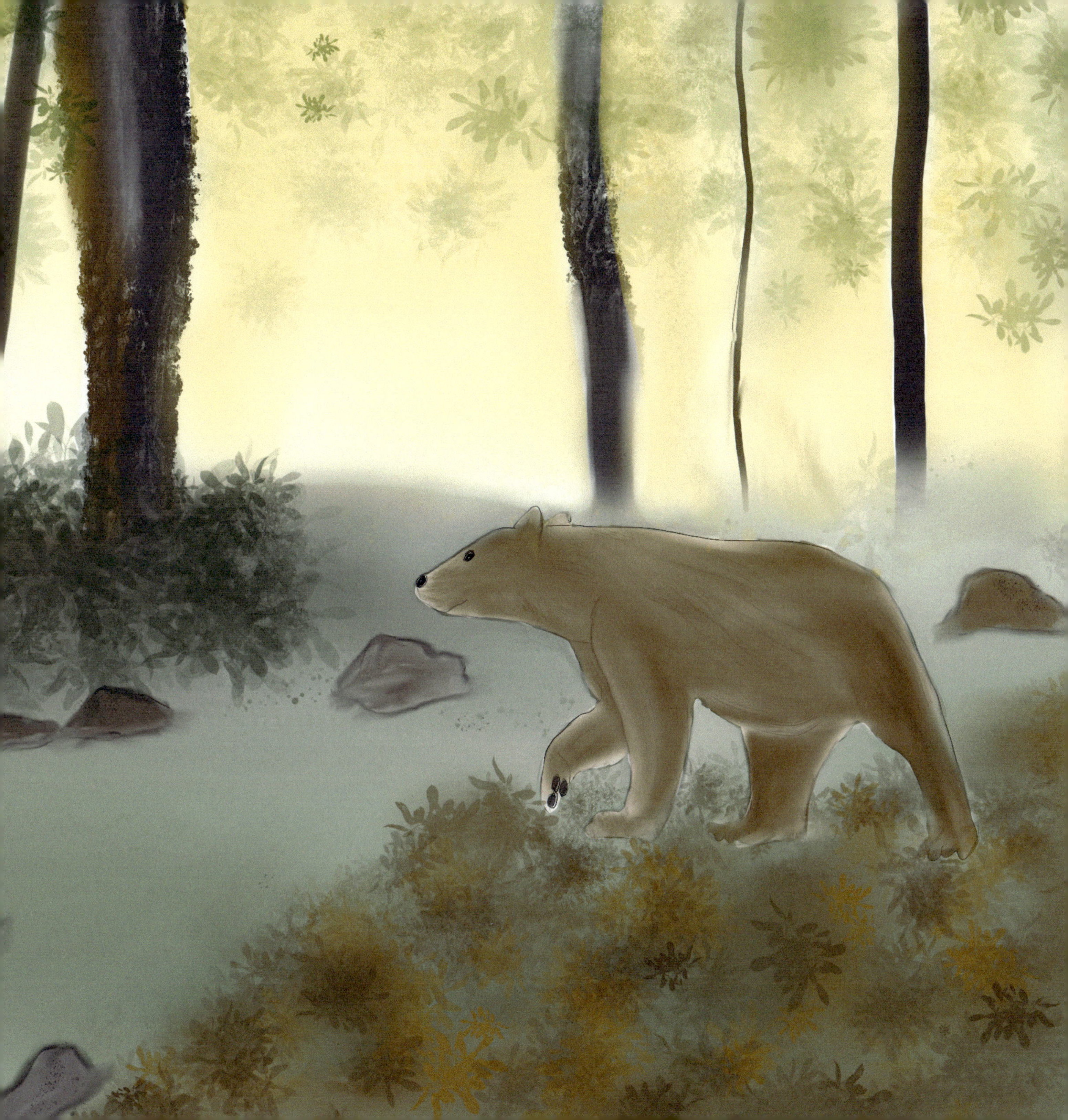

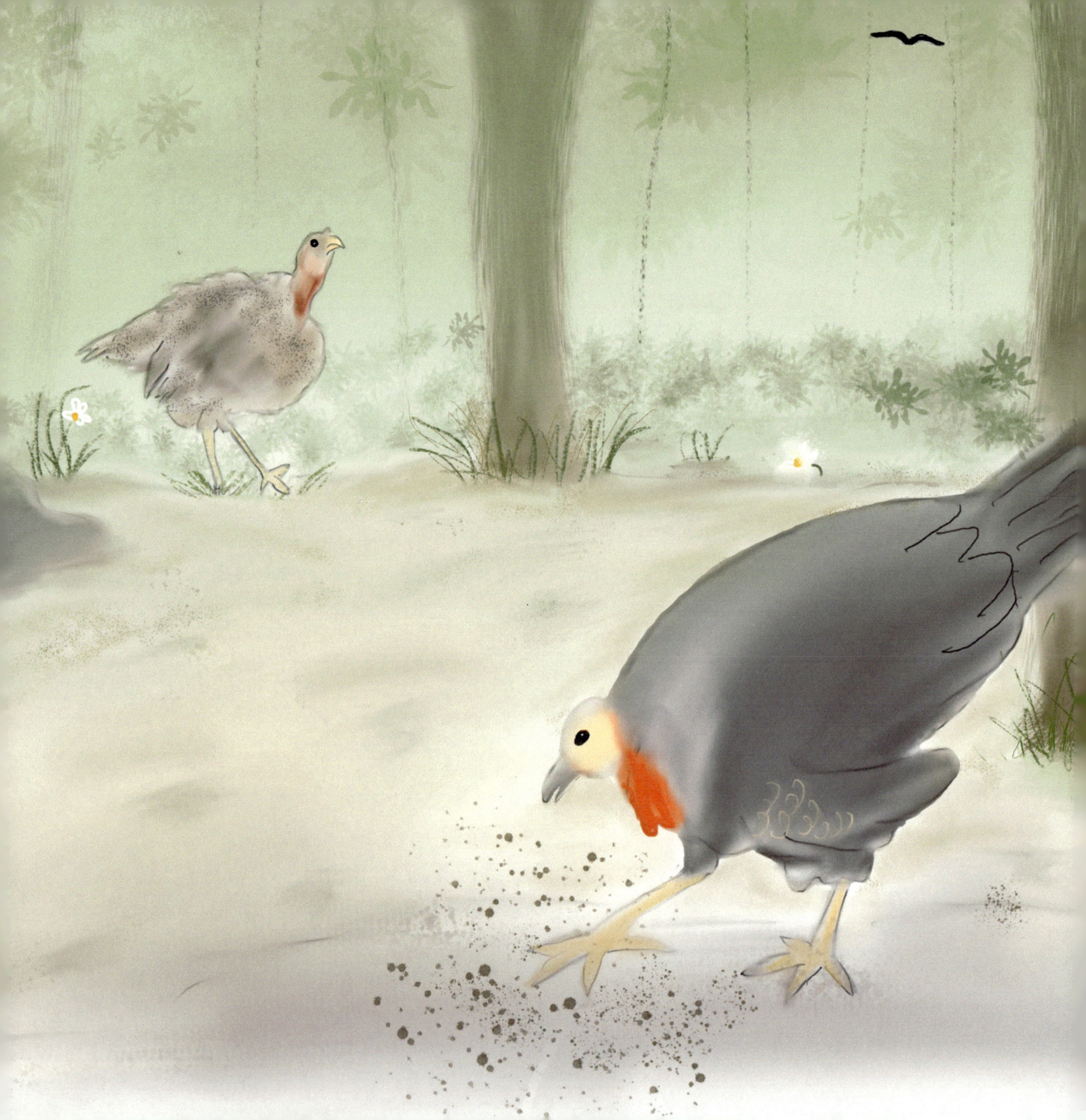

Throughout the forest
scratching on the leafy ground
I spy a turkey
eating what he has found

Throughout the forest
All around
You will find...
Big animals,
Small animals,
So many kinds...

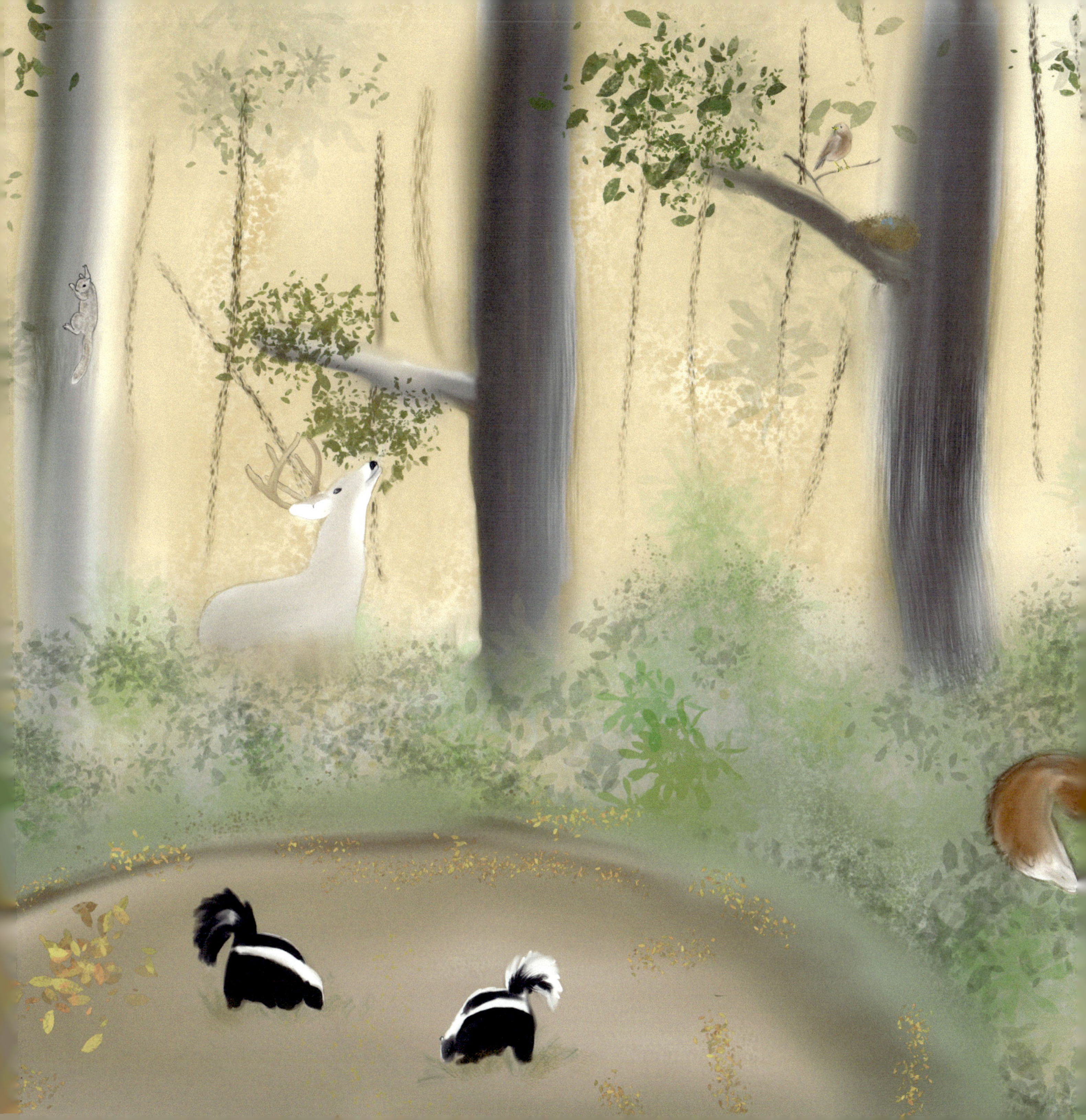

The End

Joni Prew
Circle Time Productions

I am a former early childhood educator that loves to make learning fun.

I was born in Connecticut, I graduated with a Masters in Early Childhood Education and taught elementary school children for almost 20 years. I am married to my amazing husband, Terry, and we have one daughter, Ali. I have the sweetest dog (Marley) and two crazy cats (Salem and Teddy).

I currently live in North Carolina.

When not writing or illustrating books, I enjoy golfing, gardening, hiking and crafting.

Other books in the "Animals in Natural Habitats" series

Into the Jungle
All Around the Pond
Under the Ocean
At the North and South Poles
Across the Desert

Other books by Joni Prew:

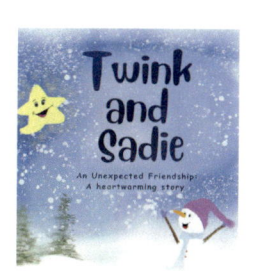

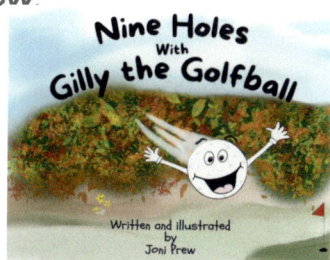

Twink and Sadie
An Unexpected Friendship:
A heartwarming story
Written and Illustrated by Joni Prew

Nine Holes With Gilly the Golfball
Written and illustrated by Joni Prew

The "Animals in Natural Habitat" series
provides lots of learning opportunities in
science, language & reading.

Visit our website for fun activities to do with each of our books.
Sign up for the CTP newsletter to get any new updates.
(I hate spam so, we promise not to spam you!)

Joni Prew
Circle Time Productions

www.circletimeproductions.com

The best compliment you can give an author or illustrator is to leave a review for their book and recommend it to others.

If you liked this book, you can leave a review on Amazon, OakieBees.com or our website www.circletimeproductions.com

Made in the USA
Columbia, SC
30 October 2024